W9-DGF-473

Global Issues

Biodiversity

Cheryl Jakab

Smart Apple Media

This edition first published in 2008 in the United States of America by Smart Apple Media.
All rights reserved. No part of this book may be reproduced in any form or by any means without written permission from the publisher.

Smart Apple Media
2140 Howard Drive West
North Mankato, Minnesota 56003

First published in 2007 by
MACMILLAN EDUCATION AUSTRALIA PTY LTD
627 Chapel Street, South Yarra, Australia 3141

Visit our Web site at www.macmillan.com.au or go directly to www.macmillanlibrary.com.au

Associated companies and representatives throughout the world.

Copyright © Cheryl Jakab 2007

Library of Congress Cataloging-in-Publication Data

Jakab, Cheryl.
    Biodiversity / by Cheryl Jakab.
    p. cm. — (Global issues)
    Includes index.
    ISBN 978-1-59920-124-5
1. Biodiversity—Juvenile literature. I. Title.

    QH541.15.B56J35 2007
    333.95'16–dc22

                                                        2007004559

Edited by Anna Fern
Text and cover design by Cristina Neri, Canary Graphic Design
Page layout by Domenic Lauricella and Cristina Neri
Photo research by Legend Images
Illustrations by Andrew Louey; graphs by Raul Diche
Maps courtesy of Geo Atlas

Printed in U.S.

Acknowledgements
The author and the publisher are grateful to the following for permission to reproduce copyright material:

Front cover inset photograph: Aerial photo of the Amazon, © Johnny Lye/Shutterstock. Earth photograph courtesy of Photodisc.

Background photograph of Earth and magnifying glass image both courtesy of Photodisc.

© Jean-Paul Ferrero/AUSCAPE, p. 12; © Pavel German/AUSCAPE, p. 15;
BigStockPhoto, p. 29; © Carolinehenri/Dreamstime.com, pp. 7 (top), 13; © Gelyngfjell/Dreamstime.com, p. 17;
© Hypedesk/Dreamstime.com, p. 14; © Kristanene/Dreamstime.com, pp. 6 (bottom), 16; © Sabobros/Dreamstime,
p. 19; © Natalia Bratslavsky/Fotolia, p. 5; © Thierry Planche/Fotolia, p. 9; © Brasil2/iStockphoto.com, p. 10;
© Ian Scott/iStockphoto.com, p. 22; NOAA, pp. 7 (bottom), 21; Photolibrary, p. 11; Photolibrary/OSF, pp. 7 (right),
25; Photolibrary/Science Photolibrary, p. 23; © Johnny Lye/Shutterstock, p. 6 (left); © J. Norman Reid/Shutterstock,
p. 18; © TAOLMOR/Shutterstock, p. 24.

While every care has been taken to trace and acknowledge copyright, the publisher tenders their apologies
for any accidental infringement where copyright has proved untraceable. Where the attempt has been
unsuccessful, the publisher welcomes information that would redress the situation.

Please note
At the time of printing, the Internet addresses appearing in this book were correct. Owing to the dynamic
nature of the Internet, however, we cannot guarantee that all these addresses will remain correct.

Contents

Facing global issues   4

What's the issue? Loss of biodiversity   5

Biodiversity issues around the globe   6

ISSUE 1
Land clearing   8

ISSUE 2
Introduced species   12

ISSUE 3
Loss of large mammals   16

ISSUE 4
Threats to ocean life   20

ISSUE 5
The threat of extinction   24

What can you do? Protect biodiversity   28

Toward a sustainable future   30

Web sites   30

Glossary   31

Index   32

Glossary words
When a word is printed in **bold**, you can look up its meaning in the glossary on page 31.

Facing global issues

Hi there! This is Earth speaking. Will you take a moment to listen to me? I have some very important things to discuss.

We must face up to some urgent environmental problems! All living things depend on my environment, but the way you humans are living at the moment, I will not be able to keep looking after you.

The issues I am worried about are:
- the huge number of people on Earth
- the supply of clean air and water
- wasting resources
- energy supplies for the future
- protecting all living things
- **global warming** and **climate change**

My global challenge to you is to find a **sustainable** way of living. Read on to find out what people around the world are doing to try to help.

Fast fact

In 2005, the **United Nations Environment Program** Report, written by experts from 95 countries, concluded that 60 percent of Earth's resources are being **degraded** or used unsustainably.

What's the issue?
Loss of biodiversity

Biodiversity is the variety of living things in a **habitat**. Biodiversity is measured by counting the number of **species** in an area. Areas with a large number of different species are said to have high biodiversity.

Today, huge numbers of species of living things are rare, **threatened**, or becoming **extinct**. The speed of this loss of biodiversity is alarming.

The importance of biodiversity

It is important to protect biodiversity because:
- biodiversity keeps Earth's **ecosystems** in balance
- Earth's **climate** is influenced by ecosystems and biodiversity
- species loss may impact other species
- species that are useful to people are being lost
- each living thing has a right to survive

Known species on Earth

The number of species identified and described by science is constantly increasing.

Earth is rich in biodiverse habitats, such as this forest in the United States.

Group of living things	Number of known species in group
Bacteria	4,000
Simple microscopic life	80,000
Vertebrates (animals with backbones)	52,000
Invertebrates (animals without backbones)	1,272,000
Fungi	72,000
Plants (flowering and nonflowering plants)	270,000
Total described species	1,750,000
Possible total (including species still to be discovered)	14,000,000

Biodiversity issues

The loss of biodiversity is due to many causes. Around the globe, issues that are affecting biodiversity include:

- land clearing leading to loss of habitats (see issue 1)
- **introduced species** pushing out local species (see issue 2)
- large **mammals** being particularly threatened or endangered (see issue 3)
- threats to ocean life in **marine** habitats (see issue 4)
- areas that are rich in species found nowhere else needing urgent protection (see issue 5)

ARCTIC OCEAN

Arctic Circle

NORTH AMERICA

New York

NORTH PACIFIC OCEAN

NORTH ATLANTIC OCEAN

Amazon

SOUTH AMERICA

of Capricorn

ATL

ISSUE 1

The Amazon
Land clearing, removing and changing natural habitats.
See pages 8–11.

ISSUE 3

Kenya
Large mammals threatened by humans. See pages 16–19.

around the globe

Fast fact
Today, plant and animal species are becoming extinct much faster than during the extinctions 64 million years ago that killed the dinosaurs.

ISSUE 2
New York
Introduced species pushing out native species. See pages 12–15.

Arctic Circle

A S I A

A F R I C A

Kenya

ISSUE 5
New Zealand
A biodiversity hot spot needing protection. See pages 24–27.

Equato

I N D I A N

TH

NTIC

O C E A N

AUSTRALIA

Tropic of Capricorn

AN

New Zealand

Antarctic Circle

ISSUE 4

Australian oceans
Overfishing and pollution. See pages 20–23.

7

Land clearing

Land clearing is removal of plants that cover the land. Today, land is being rapidly cleared to build homes, cities, and roads, to create new farmland, and to log useful timber. Land clearing is the major cause of loss of biodiversity today.

Habitat destruction

The plant covering of the land provides food and homes for living things on the land. When large areas of habitat are cleared, a decline in the number of species in that area follows.

Clearing rain forests

Land clearing in rain forests poses a serious threat to biodiversity on Earth. Rain forests have the richest biodiversity of all land habitats. They are home to about half of all known plant and animal species.

Fast fact
Most of the clearing of rain forest today occurs in Brazil, Indonesia, the Democratic Republic of the Congo, Bolivia, Mexico, Venezuela, and Malaysia.

■ Tropical rain forest areas of the world

ASIA

Tropic of Cancer

Equator

Tropic of Capricorn

SOUTH AMERICA

AUSTRALIA

DIRECTION
N
W   E
S

CASE STUDY
The Amazon rain forest

The Amazon rain forest, in South America, is the largest area of tropical rain forest in the world. It covers more than 2.3 million square miles (6 million sq km) surrounding the 3,980 miles (6,400 km) of the Amazon River.

Life in the Amazon

The Amazon is very rich in biodiversity. Much of the area has not yet been studied, and there are many species still to be discovered by scientists. A typical area of 4 square miles (10 sq km) may contain more than 1,500 plant species, 700 animal species, and thousands of insects.

Some living things from the Amazon

Plants	Animals	
palm trees	deer	monkeys
rubber trees	tapirs	anteaters
mangroves	armadillos	capybaras
ferns	freshwater dolphins	
orchids		
lianas and vines	toucans, macaws, and hummingbirds	

Fast fact

It has been estimated that of the forest lost in the Amazon, 34 percent has been used for logging roads, loading bays, and bulldozer tracks.

Despite problems of erosion, the rate of clearing in the Amazon rain forest is still rapidly increasing.

Threats

Today, damage caused by clearing for farms, logging, and fires is a serious threat to species diversity. Beginning in the 1960s, governments controlling the Amazon rain forest encouraged use of the area under the slogan, "Land without men for men without land."

Farming in cleared areas enables meat to be produced cheaply for export. However, in just a few years, cattle farming depletes nutrients in the soil and causes erosion. More land is then cleared.

Toward a sustainable future: Controlling land clearing

To protect rain forests and other ecosystems, land clearing must be controlled. However, with the human population increasing rapidly, there is great demand for land. What is left of natural habitat needs to be protected.

Parks in the rain forest

Setting aside areas of natural habitat as parks or reserves is vital to maintaining rain forests and other ecosystems. Parks in Brazil's rain forest include the fairly small Amazonia National Park, established in 1974. The largest national park in the world is the Tumucumaque National Park, created in 2002. This huge area of largely uninhabited Amazon rain forest may still not be enough to protect the biodiversity there.

Fast fact

Many scientists predict that all tropical rain forest systems will be destroyed by 2030 if **deforestation** continues at the present rate.

Valuing natural habitat

The whole Earth community must protect natural habitats, particularly rain forests. This means not simply forcing conservation on locals, but encouraging people everywhere to support them. The problem of conserving rich natural habitats must be seen as a global problem to be given global attention.

Could tourism help save the Amazon rain forest?

Yanomami Indians collect food from the Amazon forest.

CASE STUDY
Tumucumaque National Park

The Tumucumaque National Park, in the northern Amazon, covers 14,940 square miles (38,700 sq km), an area the size of Switzerland. The park contains many unidentified and rare species.

Conservation costs money

The creation of national parks is not always enough to conserve biodiversity in the area. Protecting the rain forest can be difficult, especially when wealthy countries keep up demand for rain forest products. Illegal logging, mining, and animal collecting are common in Brazilian national parks. The Brazilian government employs people to look after parks, but does not have enough money to do the job well.

A helping hand

Tumucumaque National Park is being created with the participation of the World Wildlife Fund and other international environmental groups. With international funding, it is hoped that the park will successfully protect the precious biodiversity of this area.

Fast fact
The second largest National Park in the world is Salonga National Park, in the Democratic Republic of the Congo, which covers 13,900 square miles (36,000 sq km).

Introduced species

Introduced species are living things brought from their native area and introduced into new habitats. Introduced species are a serious threat to biodiversity worldwide. Some introduced species survive and reproduce quickly to become **pests**, threatening farmland and natural habitat.

The spread of introduced species

Species deliberately taken by people to new areas include farm animals and plants, garden plants, animals for pets, and animals for hunting. Some species are also spread by accident, including mice and rats, many insects, fungi, and even viruses.

Fast fact

Some introduced animal pests include:
- African bees in South America
- Argentinian ants worldwide
- cane toads in Australia
- European wasps in Australia and New Zealand
- marine snails in Hawaii
- opossums in New Zealand
- rabbits in Australia
- zebra mussels in ship ballast worldwide

Pests

Today there are few environments on Earth not changed by introduced pests. Some introduced species do not survive in their new habitats. Others increase to huge numbers and become pests. Many species introduced as garden plants and animal pets have escaped and become a problem.

In Australia, these introduced rabbits compete for food with native animals such as wallabies.

Starlings are causing the decline of native birds.

CASE STUDY
Starlings in New York

A well-known example of a deliberate introduction gone wrong is the common starling in the United States. Starlings are lively birds which feed on any plant or animal food eaten by other birds. They nest in holes, cavities in trees, or on buildings, and often take over the nests made by other birds. The starling is now a serious threat to native birds.

Introducing the starling

In 1890, a manufacturer named Eugene Scheiffelin decided that New York should be home to all songbirds mentioned in works by William Shakespeare. Scheiffelin released 100 starlings into Central Park. By 1942, starlings had bred rapidly and spread across America.

A worldwide problem

The common starling is now a pest in North America, Australia, New Zealand, South Africa, Mexico, and the West Indies. Many native birds are under pressure because of competition from starlings and other introduced species, as well as other human influences on habitats.

Fast fact
Every three months, a new species is added to San Francisco Bay, in California, named the worst area in the world for introduced species.

Toward a sustainable future: Controlling pests

Despite awareness of the problems of introduced species, new introductions continue to occur. In particular, more air and sea travel around the world are increasing the spread of pest species.

Control strategies

Work on controlling introduced species includes:

- reducing weed invasions by constant removal of **exotic species** before they flower and spread, and replacing weeds with native species
- developing methods to reduce the risk of accidental transportation of foreign species
- controlling future deliberate introductions with the utmost care by testing to see if they will become pests before introduction is made
- working on new biological control measures that do not have any damaging effects on other species
- educating people to help prevent the accidental transport of foreign species

Fast fact
About half of all species known to have become extinct were species living on islands affected by introduced pests.

Cane toads became pests in Australia when they were introduced to try to control beetles that were damaging sugarcane.

This feral cat is eating a young bridled nailtail wallaby, an endangered species.

CASE STUDY

Introduced pets in Australia

In Australia, many pet animals, such as cats and dogs, are introduced species. Cats and dogs are hunting animals and are a threat to native wildlife.

Natural hunters

Small mammals, frogs, lizards, insects, and birds are all food to cats and dogs. Many Australian native animals are not well adapted to avoiding these skilled hunters. Cats and dogs often escape or are released into the wild, where they live by hunting. These feral animals can be a major problem for native animals.

Controlling pets

In many areas in Australia, people are encouraged to control their pets to stop them from damaging wildlife. Some areas have regulations aimed at preventing damage from pets. For example, stopping cats from roaming at night can prevent them from killing native animals. Some local councils have cat curfew laws or bans on cats roaming at any time.

Fast fact

The Australian Nature Conservation Agency estimates that the average domestic cat kills about 25 native animals a year. This means that about 75 million native animals are destroyed by domestic cats each year.

15

Loss of large mammals

Large land mammals have particular survival problems:

- They need large areas of habitat.
- They need to be protected from being hunted.
- Many of these animals are hunters themselves, and the food that they need may not be available in changing habitats.

Fast fact
In the Congo, hunting of hippopotamuses for meat and ivory has led to their decline from more than 30,000 in 1994 to less than 2,000 in 2006.

Tigers, elephants, and other fascinating large mammals were the main focus of early animal conservation. Even with the great interest in saving them, numbers of most large mammals are still seriously low worldwide.

Large animals need large habitats

The amount of available habitat is often not enough to support sustainable populations of large animals.

Pressure from people

In areas where many people rely on farming and hunting to make a living, large land animals are experiencing increasing pressure from hunting, and from competition for land.

Around the world, habitats of large animals, such as tigers in Asia, are becoming increasingly reduced in size and degraded.

CASE STUDY
African elephants

The African elephant once roamed the entire continent of Africa. These abundant elephant populations have now declined to groups in scattered areas south of the Sahara.

Fast fact
In 1989, when elephants were added to the international list of the most endangered species, there were less than 1 percent of their original number. Today it is estimated about half that number survive.

Reasons for decline

Trade in ivory has been a major cause of the decline in numbers of elephants throughout the 1900s. **Desertification** continues to threaten the tiny remaining populations that are mainly in national parks or reserves. Habitat turning to **desert** led to the total disappearance of elephants in North Africa.

Elephant numbers in Africa	
Year	**Number**
1930	5 to 10 million
1979	1.3 million
1989	600,000
2003	300,000

Current threats

Illegal ivory trade still poses a threat to remaining unprotected elephants. Although herds are thriving in some reserves, their large food demand is causing serious ecological damage, which threatens many other African species. Habitat loss and degradation are the major threats to survival, along with increasing competition from people for land.

Poachers kill elephants for their ivory tusks.

Toward a sustainable future: Setting aside habitat

Huge areas need to be set aside to provide suitable habitat for large mammals to survive. Setting aside these areas also provides a home for other living things, protecting much more biodiversity than just the large mammals.

Sustaining population

Protected areas must be large enough to provide for the needs of animals and protect them from hunting and poaching. Sometimes, if numbers of mammals increase, it may be necessary to control their numbers by culling, using birth control, or moving animals to other areas. In this way, the habitat can continue to support the population.

Large animals can be dangerous to people, but still need protection.

Captive breeding

Captive breeding programs are used when the number of a species falls dangerously low. In captive breeding, the few surviving species are bred in zoos and reserves and then released into safe habitat in the wild.

Fast fact

CITES (The Convention on International Trade in Endangered Species of Wild Fauna and Flora) is designed to protect endangered species by making trade of their products illegal. For example, a 1989 CITES ban on ivory was supported by over 120 countries. This ban diminished the illegal ivory trade and reduced the killing of elephants.

CASE STUDY
The giant panda

In the early 2000s, about 1,600 giant panda survived in the wild. China and the World Wildlife Fund are working together to save the giant panda from extinction. Wild pandas are still one of the most seriously endangered species in the world.

Fast fact
Pandas were classified as an endangered species in the 1980s, and are on the **World Conservation Union**'s Red List of Threatened Animals.

Threats to survival

Threats to survival of giant pandas include:
- a decrease in areas of habitat
- risk of starvation from loss of food in bamboo die-off
- low numbers leading to inbreeding and an increase in inherited diseases

Conservation

Since 1998, bans on logging have helped protect most panda habitat. Extensive reforestation of poor quality farmland is also creating new panda habitat.

Other conservation strategies include:
- replanting or preserving bamboo, the food that pandas eat
- expanding existing reserves and creating new reserves
- controlling poaching
- ceasing the taking of wild pandas by zoos
- restocking pandas in the wild through captive breeding programs

Pandas are still endangered, even with all the help they are getting from conservation groups.

Threats to ocean life

Oceans cover about 70 percent of Earth's surface. They provide a range of habitats, from shorelines and reefs to open ocean and the deep-sea floor. Each habitat has different ecosystems with different life forms, many of which have never been seen or studied.

Damage to ocean life

Many species in all ocean habitats are threatened, including many fish species taken for human food. Fish, corals, snails, crustaceans, and other invertebrate groups are suffering and in decline.

Human activity is threatening all life zones in the oceans, with coastal areas under the most pressure. Threats to biodiversity in marine habitats around the world include:

- overuse by people, especially by overfishing using huge nets
- pollution from industry, agriculture, and cities
- global warming, with increased sea temperatures changing habitat conditions

Fast fact
Throughout the world, many fish species including halibut, herring, cod, salmon, anchovies, sardines, and some tuna are now severely affected by overfishing.

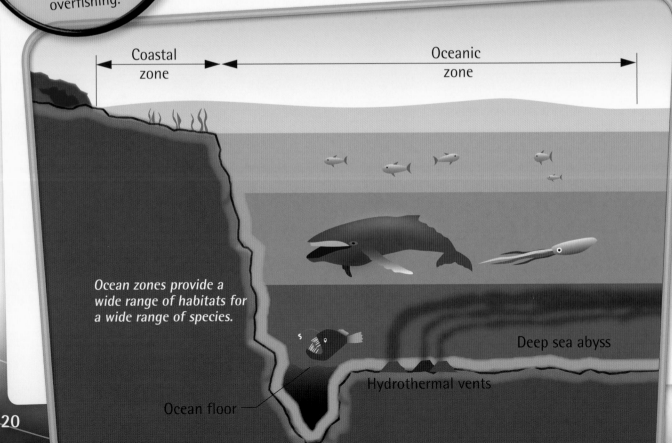

Coastal zone

Oceanic zone

Ocean zones provide a wide range of habitats for a wide range of species.

Deep sea abyss

Hydrothermal vents

Ocean floor

CASE STUDY

Overfishing of southern bluefin tuna

Southern bluefin tuna is an important commercial fish in Australia. In summer, large numbers come to waters off the southern Australian coast. Like oceans all over the world, Australian waters are being overfished. In 2006, the southern bluefin tuna was listed as a threatened species.

Increased fishing

The total world catch of southern bluefin tuna more than tripled in the 1950s and 1960s. The largest catch ever taken was about 80,000 tons in one year, in the early 1960s. The catches then levelled off, largely because of decreased fish available due to pollution and overfishing.

Limits on catches have now been set in Australia. However, the total world catch of tuna is still about 17,000 tons per year. This level of fishing allows southern bluefin tuna little chance of rebuilding to sustainable numbers.

Southern bluefin tuna can live for 40 years, reach a weight of 440 pounds (200 kg), and measure 6.5 feet (2 m) in length.

Fast fact

Coral reefs of the world are now at risk due to pollution and global warming. Some predictions suggest two-thirds of the reefs may die in the next 30 years.

Toward a sustainable future: Protecting the oceans

Damage to ocean habitats and life usually attracts little popular interest, apart from whales and coral reefs. Biodiversity in oceans can be protected by:

- setting aside **marine parks**
- controlling fishing levels
- decreasing pollution

Marine parks and reserves

Setting aside adequate areas of marine parks and reserves protects all the species in the area, not just the few that are seen from the surface. It is important that breeding areas are protected and that places with different species, marine zones, and ecosystems are made into parks.

Controlling fishing

Fish is an important source of food. Fish stocks, however, need to be protected from overfishing if they are to continue to survive. An important step is for consumers to think about the source of their fish. Fish farming is one way to provide fish with less impact on natural environments.

Fast fact

More than 70 percent of Earth's surface is covered by oceans, yet only 0.5 percent of the world's oceans are protected.

Marine parks like the Great Barrier Reef World Heritage Area help conserve biodiverse marine habitats.

CASE STUDY
Whaling

Fast fact
There is no product gained from whales that cannot be replaced by other sources.

Whales are highly intelligent marine mammals. Most of the commercially valuable whale species are now endangered. Whaling is the main cause of decline in whale numbers.

The International Whaling Commission (IWC) regulates whaling by:
- setting limits on where whaling occurs and how many are taken
- banning the hunting of rare and endangered species

Whale species	Estimated number in the Southern Hemisphere today
Blue	Fewer than 2,000
Fin	Around 20,000
Sei	No agreed estimates
Southern right	Between 7,000 and 8,000 (90 percent decline in numbers)
Sperm	No agreed estimates—seriously depleted in the 1800s
Minke	No agreed estimates—over 100,000 in the North Atlantic

Proposed whale sanctuary

In 2000, the Australian and New Zealand governments proposed the establishment of a South Pacific Whale Sanctuary to the IWC, to protect the breeding grounds of whales in the Southern Ocean. This attempt to prohibit whaling failed to achieve the required majority of IWC votes.

Japan and Norway conduct whaling today. Conservation groups such as Greenpeace continue to fight for a total ban on whaling.

A southern right whale with her calf.

The threat of extinction

The recent rate of extinction of species around the world is alarming. In 2006, another 784 species were declared extinct. The problem is getting worse, as a wide range of habitats, from deserts to rain forests and arctic lands, are now threatened.

Red List of Threatened Species

In 2006, the World Conservation Union assessed over 40,000 species across the globe and found that more than 16,000 species were threatened with extinction. Many more species not on the "Red List" are being lost before they have even been assessed.

Biodiversity hot spots

Some areas have been identified as being home to a wide range of species that occur nowhere else on Earth. The combined area of these "biodiversity hot spots" is less than 3 percent of the Earth's land surface. Protecting biodiversity hot spots can help protect a large number of species from the threat of extinction.

This red-ruffed lemur lives in Madagascar, a "biodiversity hot spot."

Fast fact

The dodo of Mauritius has become the symbol of extinction. This shy, flightless bird was wiped out by hunting in 1681, less than 100 years after it was first seen by Europeans.

The kakapo is a large, flightless parrot that is only found in New Zealand.

CASE STUDY

The New Zealand "life raft"

New Zealand is like an ancient life raft of biodiversity. New Zealand has been cut off from other land for many millions of years, leaving these islands with a large number of plants and animals found nowhere else. Since New Zealand was colonized by people about 700 years ago, many species have been lost.

Diverse habitats and strange birds

New Zealand habitats range from subtropical in the north to almost frozen in the south. Many flightless birds evolved on New Zealand including the kiwi, kakapo, and the now extinct moa. The lack of predators before the coming of humans meant that living on the ground was safe for these flightless birds.

Threats to flightless birds

Many of New Zealand's flightless birds are unafraid of humans. This characteristic became deadly when hunters arrived. Today, many flightless birds only survive on offshore islands where they are safe from predation by stoats, rats, and cats. Sixty-three bird species in New Zealand are today threatened with extinction due to introduced predators.

Fast fact
In 2006, the World Economic Forum rated New Zealand best in the world on the Environmental Performance Index.

Toward a sustainable future: How to protect more species

When huge numbers of species are threatened with extinction, working out how to save as many species as possible is difficult. Work continues on saving well-loved individual species such as elephants, pandas, and whales. But it may be more effective to set aside habitat rather than only focusing on individual species.

Setting aside ecosystems

The huge numbers of species at risk, along with declining habitat, mean choices need to be made. Over 50 percent of plants and 42 percent of vertebrate animals live in 34 identified "biodiversity hot spots" around the globe. Immediate protection of these hot spots by making them reserves or parks would save whole communities of living things from extinction.

Fast fact

Most of the biodiversity of Earth is not in the large species we can see, but in the tiny life forms that go unnoticed in the soil and in water.

Setting aside habitat in these biodiversity hot spots would save many species.

NORTH AMERICA

California Floristic Province

Madrean Pine-Oak Woodlands

Mesoamerica

Caribbean Islands

Tumbes-Chocó-Magdalena

Cerrado

Tropical Andes

SOUTH AMERICA

Atlantic Fore

Chilean Winter Rainfall-Valdivian Forests

CASE STUDY
The United Nations Plant Diversity Project

The United Nations Plant Diversity Project aims to protect at least 50 percent of the most important areas of plant diversity across the globe. Protection of the named 34 biodiversity hot spots as reserves or parks will help save the habitat of a large part of Earth's plant biodiversity.

What is a hot spot?

To be designated as a hot spot, an area must have at least 1,500 species of plants found nowhere else. The list of hot spots is published as a guideline and to put pressure on countries to give these ecosystems priority in conservation efforts.

Effective planning to protect biodiversity needs to be global. However, individual countries are responsible for their own biodiversity. In the interests of global biodiversity, **developing countries** will need support from the global community. The hot spot list has had a huge impact on directing conservation funds to areas rich in biodiversity.

Fast fact
The biodiversity hot spot concept was defined by the British ecologist Norman Myers in 1988.

EUROPE

Caucasus

Mountains of Central Asia

ASIA

Mediterranean Basin

Irano-Anatolian

Himalaya

Mountains of Southwest China

Japan

Indo-Burma

AFRICA

Eastern Afromontane

Horn of Africa

Philippines

inean Forests West Africa

Western Ghats and Sri Lanka

Coastal Forests of Eastern Africa

Sundaland

Wallacea

East Melanesian Islands

Madagascar and the Indian Ocean Islands

Polynesia-Micronesia

Succulent Karoo

AUSTRALIA

New Caledonia

Cape Floristic Region

Maputaland-Pondoland-Albany

Southwest Australia

New Zealand

DIRECTION

N
W   E
S

What can you do?
Protect biodiversity

You may think that just one person cannot do much, but everyone can help. If every person is careful, the little differences can add up.

Prevent loss of species

Protecting biodiversity and preventing loss of species are big issues for people to face. You can make a difference to biodiversity by:

- encouraging your family to buy wood and paper products made from plantation timber, not rain forest timber
- controlling your pet dog or cat so it does not hurt wildlife
- removing introduced weed species from your garden
- buying dolphin-friendly fish products
- not buying souvenirs with bird feathers or ivory
- visiting a zoo to learn more about wildlife protection

Fast fact
Frogs and lizards can be attracted to your garden by adding some rocks and a small pond or water feature.

Eat biodiverse foods

The foods you grow, buy, and eat can help increase biodiversity. Check your food intake to find how many different species are in your diet.

Fast fact
Seed saver networks are groups devoted to saving seeds of traditional and unusual plants to help conserve their variety.

Biodiversity of human food

There are over 20,000 known edible plants in the world. In the past, humans regularly used about 2,000 of these species as food.

Today, only a very small range of plants and animals is used as food. Varieties of rice grown in most Asian countries have dropped from thousands to about ten. Few animal species are farmed for food today because farmers use only those animals that grow quickly and provide high yields.

Try some different foods

You could try some different foods by:

- visiting a grocery store to buy some unusual fruits, vegetables, nuts, and seeds
- finding out about **indigenous** food plants in your area
- trying recipes with ingredients you do not usually use
- buying heirloom or wild varieties of vegetable seed to grow your own vegetables

Try some new fruits and vegetables at the grocery store.

Toward a sustainable future

Well, I hope you now see that if you accept my challenge your world will be a better place. There are many ways to work toward a sustainable future. Imagine it . . . a world with:

- a stable climate
- clean air and water
- nonpolluting, **renewable** fuel supplies
- plenty of food
- resources for everyone
- healthy natural environments

This is what you can achieve if you work together with my natural systems.

We must work together to live sustainably. That will mean a better environment and a better life for all living things on Earth, now and in the future.

Web sites

For further information on biodiversity, visit these Web sites:
- Center for Applied Biodiversity Science at Conservation International http://www.biodiversityhotspots.org
- Pandas International http://www.pandasinternational.org/
- Red List of Threatened Species http://www.iucnredlist.org/

Glossary

climate
the pattern of weather conditions in an area over the year

climate change
changes to the usual weather patterns in an area

deforestation
removal or clearing of forest cover

degraded
run down or reduced to a lower quality

desert
area of low plant cover and low rainfall

desertification
turning an area into desert, with low plant cover and a high risk of erosion

developing countries
countries with less developed industry, a poor economy, and a lower standard of living

ecosystems
communities of living things and their physical environments

exotic species
a species that is not native to an area

extinct
a species with no living examples left

global warming
an increase in the average temperature on Earth

habitat
the area used by a living thing to provide its needs

indigenous
from a particular area

introduced species
a non-native species brought from elsewhere

mammals
animals with backbones and hair that feed their young on milk from the mother's body

marine
to do with the oceans and salt water

marine parks
areas of coast and ocean set aside to conserve the ecology, which may be made of no-take areas, and areas of use, including sustainable fishing

pests
species that have become a problem in an area

renewable
a resource that can be constantly supplied and which does not run out

species
living things of the same grouping

sustainable
a way of living that does not use up natural resources

threatened
species under threat of extinction

tropical forest
areas of forest with high temperatures and high rainfall that are found near the Equator

United Nations Environment Program
a program, which is part of the United Nations, set up to encourage nations to care for the environment

World Conservation Union
one of the world's oldest international conservation organizations, established in France in 1948

Index

A
Africa   6–7, 16, 17
Amazon rain forest   6, 9, 10, 11
Australia   7, 21

B
biodiversity   5
biodiversity hot spots   6–7, 8, 24, 26–7

C
captive breeding   18, 19
conservation parks   10–11, 18, 22, 26, 27
Convention on International Trade in Endangered Species   18
coral reefs   21

D
desertification   17
dodo   24

E
elephants (African)   17
endangered species   6–7, 17, 19, 23, 24
erosion   9
extinction   5, 7, 14, 24–6

F
fish farming   22
fishing   7, 20, 21, 22
flightless birds (New Zealand)   25
food species   29
forest fires   9

G
global warming   20, 21

H
habitat destruction   8, 16, 17, 19
hunting big game   16, 17, 19

I
international cooperation   11, 18, 23, 27
International Whaling Commission   23
introduced species   6–7, 12–15, 25

L
land clearing   6, 8–10, 16
loss of biodiversity   8

M
mammals (large)   6, 16, 23
marine life   6–7, 20–3
marine parks   22

N
national parks   10, 11
New Zealand   7, 25

O
overfishing   7, 20, 21

P
pandas   19
pest control   14
pets   15

R
rain forest   8, 9, 10
Red List of Threatened Species   24

S
southern bluefin tuna   21
species numbers   5, 23
starlings   13
sustainable living   4, 28–9, 30

T
Tumucumaque National Park   10, 11

U
United Nations   4
United Nations Plant Diversity Project   27
United States   6–7, 13

W
whaling   23

64662S433